13 Fiddler Street

This book is a work of fiction. Any references to historical events, real people or real paces are used fictitiously. Other names, characters, places and events are products of the author's imagination. And any resemblance to actual events or places or persons, living or dead is entirely coincidental.

Contents

13 Fiddler Street

In the beginning

It was true, I had flipped the bird at most of the places I had worked. Why should anyone have to put up with complete idiots telling you what to do and I was no exception? Did it do me any good? Of course not, but I didn't mind taking a hit now and then, it was such a pleasure to release myself from the burden of working for them.

It all started during the recession, my mum and dad got together and started producing children. Looking back it seems to me to be totally irresponsible to say the least as there was a run on the banks at the time and local companies were going into liquidation all over the place. The future looked bleak.

They eventually moved into Fiddler Street, number thirteen as luck would have it and that was where we hailed from. Not the best of starts for anyone, but it was home. It wasn't long after that our dad decided that the grass was greener on the other side of the street and got himself fixed up with that blonde floozy Rita from number nine.

This little episode was the talk of the street for ages. The gossips and we know who they were, had a field day, our family was the talk of the town. Well that's gossips for you, nothing else to do, but put people down and the ones along our street were good at it.

There was that old baggage next door to us and her daughter in-law on the other side, we were like the meat in a sandwich and they would talk about us across our back garden.

Well then things with my dad moved on apace and the two of them shacked up together in number nine. After a while of concealing themselves as an item they would walk brazen faced up the street together, without a thought for our poor old mum struggling on her own to bring us kids up.

They made a handsome couple so one old boy told me many years later. Her with her bottle blonde hair, big tits and that imitation Leopard skin fur coat that she would wear even on the warmest of days. Stiletto heels along with fishnet tights, well you can imagine. Couple this with the IQ of a dead sheep and you can see just what that was all about.

I suppose the neighbours with their continuous comments must have played a part in putting the pressure on them, because a few months later they decided to move to another part of the country leaving us in peace. At last my mum could walk along the street without having to wonder if she was going to bump into the pair of them.

My name is Jim Brenner and we are the Brenner's from 13 Fiddler Street. I do have two brothers and a sister Rosy, we don't talk about her much these days as she decided to get mixed up with that bloke John Sparrow down on the Riverside Walk apartments and now thinks she's

too posh to even talk to the likes of us. What John doesn't know is that she was on the game down along the riverside walk with that blonde floozy Rita from across the street.
Two of John Sparrow's mates live just along the road from us. Charlie Watts and James Sheen, they're the ones that have the big posh shiny cars parked outside. We all wonder where that lot get their money from, because it's not from working, that's for sure.

My older brother Kenny is still in prison serving ten years for armed robbery. We all knew he was framed and it was one of John Sparrow's mates over the road that was responsible. Which one? Well we're not too sure, but one of them. That only leaves my youngest brother Dougy, short for Douglas. Well to say we had trouble from him from the start would be an understatement to say the least, he has caused the whole family grief at different times. Least of all when he got done for that arson job over on the trading estate.

We all knew he was innocent of any crime as he was overseas at the time, or so he said. He is now out on parole and says he is never going back and has turned over a new leaf becoming an entrepreneur selling stuff out of the back of his motor at night. Something he learned on one of those prison training courses they ran in the evenings. What he sold, he wouldn't tell us, but things are going very well according to his pregnant girlfriend Monica, who used to be a slapper down on the riverside walk.

Now for me Jim Brenner. I always felt ashamed when my brothers got caught for anything as it showed a severe lack of intelligence. There were a few moments that things for me got too hot to handle and I had to make a run for it myself. Take for instance the time I nearly got caught up on the roof of the local Methodist church. I had stripped all the lead off and rolled the lot up, but I had forgotten how heavy it was and had to abandon it when my bike wheels buckled under its weight. I found myself technically challenged on more than one occasion.

Well that's the Brenner's for you. All educated at the comprehensive just around the corner.

It had to be done

I had a good selection of sharp knives at my disposal, collected up from my various employments in the butchery trade. These were now being put to good use in completing this utterly unpleasant task that I had bestowed upon myself. Was I looking forward to it? Well the answer to that is no, not a bit. The problem was of my own making, when you get involved with these sort of things then there is always a downside and this morning was the culmination of events that I had gotten myself into and I was going to be terrified to say the least.

There was a slight popping sound as the knife slipped through the skin and into her stomach which caught me off guard for the moment. I had been overtaken by the nervous shaking long before I had selected my implement, this was to be my first attempt. It had started with severe twitching in my fingers and which was by now creeping up my arms and into my back affecting my shoulders. My head was completely somewhere else and a certain numbness had changed places with my brain.

She couldn't have been any more than about thirty five years old or so and it seemed such a shame to even do this kind of thing to such a pretty woman. Her face was still covered over as I tried to figure out the best way to go about this. It just wasn't me at all to get tied up in such activities as the thing that lay before me, but I needed to get this done.

The first thing to hit me was the smell and the blood, I just wasn't prepared for it. Never expecting in my wildest dreams to be in this situation in the first place, but I was and it was here and now. The sweat was dripping off my brow faster than I could mop it up and running into my eyes creating more problems as I tried to remember from that book what the next move was. The knife was well in and I proceeded to pull the thing upwards towards the top of her ribcage in as straight a line as possible. On reaching the point where the internal bones stopped any forward movement of the knife I then knew it was time to stop and consider things a little further. "I think that part was right." I said to myself more than once.

Now the next job to do was to split the ribcage open and then it was on to removing a few of the organs. In what order I didn't have had a clue, but I was to remove all of them and place them in the stainless container on the side, ready for disposal, that's what we agreed to in the first place.

The small stench filled room had driven me to a point of desperation. I was feeling decidedly sick as I picked up the rib cutter and placed it under her ribcage for the final part of this unwanted thing I had talked myself into. I will never forget the crunching sound it made as those heavy steel blades bit home and cut though. This was followed immediately by bouts of light headedness that were starting to take me over, reducing me to uncontrollable spasms as I momentarily passed out.

I brought myself back on target by remembering that cement factory and the things that went on there in the gypsum mill and I knew that some of them were still alive when they were thrown in. I had heard the screams above the noise alright and their kicking legs as they were drawn into those massive rollers, a sound I will never forget.

I drove myself forward with the words, we need to press on and get this job done. “Right, let’s have a look at things.” I heard myself say as the knife once again pressed home on what looked like some kind of artery connected to the heart. The top artery was by now free and I looked for the lower artery, even I with my poor knowledge of anatomy I realised there had to be at least two connections, in and out.

The heart at last was free and I drew it out of the cavity, not before I squirted myself with blood from squeezing it too hard and placed it onto the side of the table

I had managed everything in my life and overcome all of the obstacles until today with the traumatic experience of this morning being left here alone with this little lot on my plate. I had reached a point where I could do no more and decided to make a cup of tea and try to eat my sandwiches.

I thought back again to Dermot and Patrick in the cement factory and the friendly times we had in there. They were both asylum seekers and spoke reasonable English. They understood me well because I was in the habit of working in noisy places and was very descriptive with my hands when I spoke. I had heard their story and how they had travelled together to reach England. They were both very keen to hear my story and would keep on until I gave it to them.

“Well boys to say that we brothers were a bit on the wild side would be an understatement, my two brothers and our sister who we don’t talk about, were well off the scale and up to all sorts of stuff. This manifested itself in my later life and to be quite honest I have never really given two shits about anything since.
I started working in a butchers shop up at the junction and got on really well. I served my time and became a full time butcher. Suddenly things changed as they always do and I was made redundant. I just gave them the finger and moved

on. For me it wasn't back to the butchery trade, there were other more interesting things to do. I studied at the college for many years to obtain my engineering qualifications and then it was off into that great big world of interesting work, or so I thought.

The first place that employed me was a small engineering company in the heart of Berkshire. In other words just down the road. It was here that I met my first characters and the memory of them will be with me forever.

The factory

Mick could tell a good story and he went on this day telling me about some of his engineering experiences. Friday afternoon fun as he called it.

Mick was a very quiet sort of a guy and wouldn't say boo to a goose, but when he'd had a few drinks his evil dark side would emerge. It was as if he suppressed it all up until then, but when he started it was the best we ever heard and he really could tell them. His favourite start to any story would be as such. "Now here we have a small engineering company in the heart of

Berkshire, have you ever seen a fuck up quite like it in your entire life?" All spoken with a Scottish accent.

This small engineering company was owned by an ex-army Colonel, his right hand man was a very good engineer called Fatty, on account of his rotund body.

Mick was the foreman, but not as you might say one of the team. They kept him on the outside, but welcomed him on their Friday dinnertime drinking spree up at the local pub.

Returning late in the afternoon all the worst for wear, the three of them would struggle across the car park and back to work. The Colonel with his neatly trimmed moustache would stagger around giving the orders, none of which made any sense. Fatty would have none of this and would be spread eagled in the office waiting for his bodily functions to tell him it was time to visit the toilet.

Now the toilet block was opposite the main works with the entrance door partly obscured by a storage rack. The rest of the lads always had a bet on how long he would be in there each time. The odds on favourite was half an hour at 2-1. All bets were of five minute interval, or parts thereof to stop any disputes. The main works clock to be the measure.

Right the scene was set, all eyes were on the office door.

Now this was to be a day with a difference, for some reason they had upset Mick and he was waiting his chance to get even. The office door slowly opened bellowing clouds of cigarette smoke, followed by Fatty. The time was duly noted and the bets were on. Mick announced that all bets were off as he waited for Fatty to enter the toilets and settle down. This achieved he strolled across the yard with a smouldering oily rag. Returning a few minute later with a big smile on his face.

The smoke soon billowed out of the toilet block windows amid howls of laughter. As the time passed the laughter subsided only to be replaced with concern, there had been no movement over at the toilets. Fatty they thought was choking to death.

Mick was the first to reach the toilets, his search revealed nothing, Fatty had gone. On leaving he found the door locked from the outside. His frantic waving was ignored as Fatty strolled casually back across the yard. No one went to help Mick, or really knew just what had gone on. Fatty was back in his office and Mick left later that afternoon with his cards and p45 in hand.

Mick and I had worked there together for a few years and during this time he told me another one of his stories that went down rather well at the time. This was all about his uncle Harry.

The short holiday

Harry and Kate were a dedicated middle aged couple, unfortunately they didn't have any children, whether it was down to Harry's strange ways in the bedroom, or the fact that she insisted on having the lights on during their special occasions, which were few and far between. Maybe it was due to the paper thin walls with the mother in law sleeping in the room next door. She was very frail, but with pin sharp hearing, or even that wobbly head board, one will never know.

Her incessant demands were always preceded by that sudden sound of her walking stick banging on the floor above the sitting room ceiling and could come at any moment. There was never a warning of such an event, but the command was made. Kate would jump up and attend the incident her mother demanded, this could be as little as pass me my drink. Although she was a sweet old lady her temper would flare up with the words! "I don't want to be a burden to you," if not attended to, pronto. She had been living with them for the last twenty years and things were starting to become slightly strained between the three of them.

It was decided that at last they would have a short holiday in Scotland. Kate's older sister Maureen would come over and do her bit towards her mum's care. Everything was sorted and the trip would start in a few days. Harry was over joyed at this, he and Kate could at last spend some quality time together.

The Mother in law complained that Maureen wasn't as good as Kate when it came to looking after her. These complaints increased over the next few days, then suddenly Maureen fell ill with some bug or other.

"Now what do we do Harry?" He sat there his head in his hands, plans ruined. "I'm going anyway regardless." His mind was made up. They decided that the only way was for the old lady to go with them, as another few weeks in that house with her would finish him off. Although it was a long way to travel she was tough enough they thought to make it up there easily.

The holiday started off with the long drive up to Edinburgh for the half way stage of the trip with an overnight stay. The next morning they proceeded to their final destination. A very pleasant hotel with a large veranda to the rear overlooking the gardens. Mum was more than happy resting here during the day being well attended by the hotel staff that understood the situation, while Harry and Kate went on short trips around the local area. Things were working out well for the first few days until they received a call saying that Mum had been taken ill and was being rushed to hospital.

It was dire news that greeted them on arrival, the Mother in law had passed away. The sadness hit them as this was all very sudden. A few more days and it was time to visit the undertakers to arrange things. On hearing the news Maureen insisted that mum be brought back to be buried in the family plot, as all of them were.

They were told when asked how much this would be. "You realise that the driver has to make the return trip as well, with two overnight stops." This was more money than they could afford. The undertaker did suggest that they could take her back themselves as they were going in that direction and only one way. Kate was more than upset by this, but in the end decided that the common sense of it all was the main thing.

Cutting their holiday short they collected the old lady from the undertakers and loaded her into the back of car for the return journey. The weather had been kind to them as they set off in blazing temperatures on the return journey. The smell was starting to get to them as they approached their halfway stop.

Kate had been very upset at this and needed a lot of persuasion to leave her mother in the car park all night on her own. Harry explained that it wouldn't be possible to do anything else, but could clearly understand the situation that had bestowed itself on them. The next morning taking advantage of their now freer life they decided to have a lay in. Breakfast over, they began the last homeward part, only to be overcome by fumes from the passenger.

"The only thing I can think of Kate is to put your mum up on the roof rack and the cases in here!" About the last thing that Kate wanted to hear, but after half an hour of sensible talk, she reluctantly agreed, but insisted for the sake of decency for her mother to be put up there head first. Harry had the job of lifting her up and doing the placement. He did wince slightly when tightening up the ropes as what sort of pressure to apply, it was after all his first time at this sort of thing.

The onward journey was altogether a vast improvement on the earlier part with them relaxing at last. They had wasted a lot of time that day and wanted to get home as quickly as they could, so Harry hit the floor boards.

Further south the weather started to change rapidly leaving them driving through torrential rain. This got a lot worse as they reached the county boundary, but still they pressed on regardless arriving home in a downpour.

Dashing up their drive and then in for a well-earned cup of tea, they decided to unload the car after dark.

The time came to do the deed of unloading the car! It was nice and dark by now and the rain had subsided. Harry went across the garden to where the car was parked, it was hidden from view by the tall trees and bushes. He then got the shock of his life. The roof rack had fallen off somewhere between Edinburgh and London.

"Time I suppose to go in and explain things to Kate."

I left that company a few years' later through redundancy and decided it was time to start up on my own. Something I had dreamed about for years, to be my own boss and not have to listen to others telling me what to do all of the time.

It was hard trying to maintain enough work to keep me going, but my determination to succeed was always upper most in my mind and I didn't want to fail whatever happened. Things nodded along for years and bit by bit the whole thing was starting to come together. I had regular work and the repeat orders were the thing that saved me every time.

People got to know of me and where I was and it would seem that some of them were only interested in something for nothing. Or maybe I was a soft touch for a sob story. This resulted at times in various visitors and a bloody nuisance some of them were too. "Can you do this little job for me, it won't take long, but I would appreciate it if you could do it straight away as I'm waiting to get my project finished?" The project was usually a motorcycle restoration. Being an ex-motor cyclist myself I had a certain affection for such things and anyone doing it.

There were one or two other visitors and they were the sort that hung around asking questions all of the time, bored stiff and not really having anything else to do.

It was one of these so called days that the enemy of the working man arrived.

The carpet fitter

Years ago I knew this carpet fitter guy, he was very timid in his ways and terrified of dogs. He knew that I was very adept at engineering and would on occasion visit me in my workshop. These visits were a pain to me as he would ask obvious questions. How do you do this, how do you do that?

The questions were excessive over what I could only describe a trivia. This would go on for an hour or so and all the time I just needed him to go, so I could get on.

This went on for a year or so, him wanting the answers and me trying to get rid of him without being rude. I don't have the time, or this job is behind wouldn't do it. There was something else about him, he would never believe me when I said something and would reply with a smile on his face. "No, you're having me on." I think it was something to do with the fumes off of those cheap Nylon carpets what did it!!

Then the fateful day arrived. While talking to him my wife passed the door with the dog on her way for his daily exercise. Now my dog was a goer and would growl at the slightest thing and especially carpet fitters that were terrified.

They were his favourite of all. While putting up with his tirade of questions, which went on for an hour or so my wife returned with my lovely pouch, this went unnoticed by him. He was rubbing his legs together as he asked me if he could use the toilet. I did tell him straight that it wasn't that good an idea as the dog was in there, pointing towards the kitchen door. "No, you're having me on." This went on for a while, me trying to explain that the wife had returned and him insisting that I was having him on.

He just wouldn't believe me. He reached for the kitchen door handle and started to open it, I warned him again. "Go on then see how far you get," he just smiled and proceeded towards our bathroom. This should be good I thought, just how far will he get before my Alsatian cross Labrador snappy little bugger gets him? Things were very quiet for about two seconds. The dog then must have spotted him and kicked off big time. I tell you that all sorts was going on the other side of that closed kitchen door.

I just stood there just enjoying the screams and growling, I knew he'd had it. The next thing was he was shouting my name out loud, over and over. Half the street could hear him as well. He was screaming and calling my name, in between the dogs barking.

'Now let's see where was I before he came, ah yes, just setting that machine up for the next run.' I was really enjoying this and as I am of a slightly sinister nature, I wasn't about to rush to his rescue. I did explain clearly that the dog was in there, but it fell on deaf ears, not my fault then is it.

At least five full minutes had elapsed before I gave in and I went to rescue him. On turning to climb the stairs, there was the dog clawing at the toilet door and this voice inside shouting my name screaming to be rescued. Now the thing here was that when my dog had cornered something he wasn't about to give it up easily and it took some time to pull him away from his quarry. No need to rush why should I?

Putting him somewhere safe, I slowly returned and said the coast was clear and to come down, then I returned back to my machine. He did eventually peer around the door needing assurances the dog wasn't around. He must have really wanted a pee as it was all down the front of his trousers. I have never seen anyone so frightened in my life. As he left a strange smell emanated from his rear and I was sure he had done a little more than the obvious.

Letting the dog back in I spotted my wife and daughter doubled up on the settee making strange squeaking sounds. They must have seen the funny side of it as well, I thought. After what must have been five minutes or so of these two adults being unable to explain themselves, they finally settled down enough to say that my fourteen year old daughter had been in the toilet at the time he burst in.

My daughter tells it like this: “We never lock the door as we are all family. I was in the toilet when I suddenly heard the dog going wild and footsteps racing up the stairs. Then a total stranger burst in and pushed the door shut. I just sat there while the dog tried to attack him. He faced the door all of the time. What else could he do?”

I was in my work-shop doing my sinister thing. It took a few days for that one to settle down.

We move on

My work was intermittent most of the time and it was nothing to be without work a few weeks at a time. These were the times that I had to give in and find temporary employment with others and it led on to some very strange things indeed.

Explaining my predicament one evening while talking to the landlord of my local pub resulted in the offer of some casual bar work on an ad hock basis. I had known Carlos for a few years and we got along really well. He originated from Spain and had decided to move on elsewhere in the world.

We had a lot in common as he told me one day that work back in his home country was very difficult to obtain. He took a shine to me as I had started up on my own and apparently he had tried to do the same thing back home, but he had reached the point I had with the business drying up.

So here we were again trying something new. The customers were more than pleasant, a few of them knew me and would make comments about our family, but all in a friendly sort of way. I was making friends and things were going very well. Carlos was a hands on sort of guy and would often join the regulars having a drink or two with them.

Different days would see the arrival of various groups. Today it was a get together of the mothers union and this lot took the place over like you've never seen. The drinks flowed continuously and boy could they put it away. The thing that always surprised me was the amount of noise they could make, it was continuous. Carlos was in his element looking after his little beauties as he called them.

Dinner times saw the arrival of the lads from the gas works just across the river at exactly twelve thirty. This was a busy time as they all wanted something to eat and quickly. Hot pies were their favourite and it wasn't long before we had them satisfied. They were a ragged bunch all dressed in their blue boiler suits and would pass on stories about the things that went on over in the gas works and some of them were really funny.

The working girls that frequented the riverside walk would appear in the evenings all dressed up to the nines. One or two would pick up a trick and would be off well before we knew it, earning their money. Brenda from the Riverside Café was a regular and would stop off on her way back from work to chat to them before heading home. She always looked too strong to me to be a girl, but there you have it, it takes all sorts to make a world. Jack Sparrow the rich old boy would arrive with a few of his mates Charlie and James. They would always form a huddle over in the corner and scheme their way through the evening. I knew from old that they were up to things, just what, had always eluded me.

The week-ends where completely different. The habitual drinkers would arrive at various times, some in groups, others as individuals. Then there was the occasional visit from the local tramp who we called Doogy. A sinister looking man that would shuffle along very quietly always catching me off guard as he propped himself up at the bar.

“Hi Doogy what’s your pleasure?”
“Hi Jim, my usual please, have you heard about what went on in here last Sunday?”
“Go on.” I said with some enthusiasm. It was a lot easier this bar work if you were prepared to listen, it was the best side for a story. “There were police swarming around all over the place, there must be something big going down. What, I don’t know yet, but I will find out.”

That was his way, full of mischief, but good with the information. On Sundays there were the regulars as always. Along with a group of old boys that would spend most of the morning sat in the corner laughing and joking most of the time. I asked Carlos one day what was going down over in the corner and he told me the story that one of them had relayed to him about what went on.

The pub visit

We four old boys met up as usual in the local pub. Sunday mornings seemed to arrive a lot quicker these days, it was around to that time of the week again, before we knew it.

Harry was the oldest by a mile, with Sid, Eddy and Des a little younger, by how much we didn't know, they kept that sort of thing to themselves. Using the opportunity to lie about in whenever necessary, and they did.

At the end of the day no one really knew what was what when it came to age. The conversation was the thing here, as each one would relate a story of their adventures as they called them. The stories became more and more exaggerated as the drinks were consumed. Some true and others just plain made up for the occasion. They were all enjoyable, the thing here was to dissect the wheat from the chaff.

Whatever they were, they were good, helping to pass the time and much was made of the ones that seemed to be completely too farfetched. One of the best was Sid and his blood donor experiences. Stents played a big part in their bragging as to who had the most and where. You could never be sure about these as there was no way to check, with Harry's going from three to five in one week, having forgotten the number quoted the week before, it was all good stuff.

We all donated blood at various times of the year. Sid rubbed his arm as if to say he had just had it done. “How was it then Sid,”
“I always have difficulty trying to get them to take some, all they do is sample it and then refuse to take it.” This raised our senses big time. Was this the point where we asked, or was it the time to say ah okay and enquire no further taking his thunder away. This being the extent we had reached with the stories getting more and more exaggerated. I thought give it a go, or we will never hear the end of this truly magnificent story that was just about to unfold otherwise.

“Gone on Sid what happened?” He at first refused to answer, eventually giving in when pressurised. “Well it’s like this, I have a very rare blood group and they just check the quality each time telling me it will be for the best if we just leave it in you, until we need it.”

Now this really is the point of no return, do we enquire further? A difficult one this, as he is leading us into something. Harry and Des just sat there thinking shall we give him a lead in, or cut him off. Leaving him nonplussed as we called it.

The big problem being we would never get to hear the end of the story otherwise to judge, if we chopped him up. We wouldn't want to enquire over personal family problems now, would we? The decision was made, we wanted to know the rest! "Go on Sid tell us more. When would they need to take it?" Was the only way to go?

"Well boys, it's like this, I told you of my very rare blood group and they are leaving it in me until a member of the Royal family has a serious accident." A smile of satisfaction and well-being spread across his face. This one kept us going the rest of the morning, but we all agreed it was class.

Harry was the first to speak after we regained our senses. "What do you like the most Sid, the truth or bull shit?" was his question. Sid was at first surprised that the question was even directed towards him, saying. "Oh you mean me. Well it's like this boys, if you tell the truth then you and the family only went to Brighton for a week staying in a grubby cheap hotel, but with a little bit of bull shit it's going to be three weeks on the French Riviera, now isn't it, what would you prefer, eh?" There was no real answer, as any comment would be turned around the next week and it may be difficult to escape.

If a police car passed the pub with its siren going, Harry would immediately dive under the table, surfacing only after it had passed. This made them wonder just what he had been up to. Des on the other hand had his admirers and was one for the ladies. Always over smelling of after shave, it was at times overpowering. On occasion showing us photos of models and beautiful women that he couldn't have possibly known. Harry was the more sophisticated of us, with a sinister dry sense of humour that resulted in him coming out with real gems from time to time. Even when he said something really amusing that would roll us up, his expression rarely changed.

Eddy was always travelling somewhere, he was the one with itchy feet. Turning up on a Sunday morning he was always returning from distant climes.

So there you have it, a ladies man and a bull shitter, with a dodgy past, a traveller and the straight man. The best of friends.

The phone suddenly rang amidst all of this, it was Des that snapped into action. "Yes my little petal, I will be home soon, we are just up at the Legion having a quiet drink." Harry and Sid looked at each other. The same thought running through their minds, this is nowhere near the Legion. Des carried on this conversation for a while longer, giving all sorts of excuses, most were imaginary at best. "That was my little Lula Belle, worrying about me as usual!" Shortly afterwards he rustled through his pockets trying to find something, eventually producing a picture. "There she is my little precious and what a beauty, don't you agree?"

Looking at the picture each in turn, they had shock on their faces. To say we were surprised would be an understatement. She was truly beautiful and not the sort that would even go near someone like Des, we were convinced of that. "It must be your daughter Des, you are far too old for her!"
"You're wrong that is my little Lula belle straight up no joking."

Harry started up another conversation. “Does anyone one here know anything about mind reading, only I have been reading this book on how to do it and I need to practice on one of you.” The other two looked at each other, what was going on this morning, were things going mad or what? “Come on then, I will give it a try.” Sid was up for most things. Harry put his head in his hands. “What I want you to do is concentrate on just one thing and I will then tell you what it is.”
“What sort of thing.”
“Just any old object like a bicycle or something.” Harry put his head in his hands again. Sometime went by before he announced it was a key that Sid was thinking of. “No, it was a book.”

“Think of something else this time. I need to concentrate more deeply.” After a moment or two he said that it wasn’t fair if Sid kept changing his mind. Sid shuffled his feet, in actual fact he had changed his mind from one thing to another, part way through, so he said afterwards.

Just then things were disturbed again as a stranger that was part of the Sunday gang put his head around the door. “Hiya boys.” It was Eddy

back from four weeks holiday in Australia. “How are you Eddy, long time no see?”
“What’s all this then, Harry have you got a headache?”
“No, he’s just reading Sid’s mind.” Harry concentrated again, “It’s a coin.” “That wasn’t right,” said Sid. Eddy announced that, “it was a Zip wasn’t it?” To everyone’s surprise Harry agreed that Eddy was dead on.

“How did you manage that, have you read the book?” enquired Harry. “No just said what I saw.” They were amazed. “Try it again.” Harry went into his trance once again, concentrating hard, Eddy stared into deep space. “Got it, a chair!” Harry was surprised how accurate Eddy was, “That was it again.” Eddy polished his finger nails along his sleeve, blowing the imaginary dust off and admiring them.

Another police car passed its siren blaring, Harry dived under the table again. “What have you been up to this time?” Eddy enquired. “Oh just a little deal I did way back and that lot make me nervous,” came back the reply. “What sort of deal was that then Harry that you have to hide from our friends in blue?" "I do a nice little line in Memorabilia, all the old stuff from the war. Aeroplane parts and anything I can get my hands on.

There's still a good market out there for such things and it gives me my drinking money."
"Eddy was getting somewhere at last, after all those years wondering what Harry was all about.
"Have you sold the altimeter yet?"
"No, I'm still waiting a buyer for that."
"How about guns?" Harry paused for a second before answering that question. Eventually agreeing that he had and that's what the problem was with his nerves. Explaining that they were Spitfire cannons in working order.

The phone rang, it was Lula Belle. Des responded with the truth this time, saying he was in the Jolly Anglers down by the river. The phone call ended with Des repeating, yes okay more than once. "Well that was Lula and she's collecting me in an hour or so."

The other three all turned and looked at each other. "At last we will have a chance to see if she

is as pretty as your picture."
"You sure will boys, you sure will."
"How did you meet her Des, only you are not exactly a spring chicken now are you?"
"Well it's like this, I first met her cousin Maisie and while I was going out with her I was introduced to the rest of the family.

Most of them are in show business one way or the other. As the years went on I would lose interest in one and move onto another, they didn't seem to mind, in Brazil they just like to keep it all in the family and there is no jealousy. I'm not sure what would happen if one of them met a complete stranger. That might provoke a different response, but so far so good."

A sleek black car slipped quietly into the car park, resting up waiting. The two occupants observing the comings and goings.

"So how about you Eddy, what's you modus operandi?"
"Well I do a little trading and stuff, you know the sort of thing buying and selling mainly. All honest gear you understand, nothing tricky. I have been

doing it for years, all kinds of things, coins, jewellery and such like. Things were going well until one day this guy approached me demanding that I fence off some stuff. Like a fool I went along with it, silliest thing I ever did, as the police caught me and I paid the penalty. A couple of months at her Majesty's pleasure. It happened a few more times after that and I paid again.

I didn't ever want to go down this road, the problem is the money was great and after a time you are coining it in. A lot easier than the hard selling struggle, it really was.

The pressure was the thing that got to me the most, as with just selling hard won things, you never had to worry about a knock on the door, there never was one. The fencing off was a different ball game altogether. Anyone at the door and you were through the front curtains first, checking to see who was out there, along with a squinty through the letterbox.

I travelled all over the world as a courier with these deals that was the best part. You would never know where you were off to next. Just before my last arrest they relieved me of my passport saying I could retrieve it any time after I had been sentenced. That was the best thing ever for me as without it I was no longer any good to them and that's when they left me alone.

These days I'm so careful and everything seems to be back to normal. Let's hope it continues, as the thought of going back inside doesn't please me any." They had listened to the other three and now it was Sid's turn. Sid had sat there very quietly listening to the stories of the other three.

Sid did eventually start to tell his story. "Well I haven't done anything as exciting as you lot, far from it, just ordinary stuff, so not much to tell really. I have led a very quiet life and got on with things, none of this jetting away, or meeting loads of beautiful ladies and selling stuff.

No nothing like that, all I did was to get married three times, that's all. So not very interesting is it?" The others could see from his expression that there wasn't much left to tell, so they pressed him a little harder. "Well getting married three times is a little exotic. Tell us about that then, if that's all you've got!!"

"Okay, well it was like this, my first wife was really nice, but things started to wear off after a while a bit like Des and Maisie. Then out of the blue I met my true love, we got hitched within a few weeks. For about three years things were going well, until the beautiful one appeared. Des knows what I mean, you just can't help yourself. She wanted me and likewise. It all happened again and that's where we are to this very day. That's the problem!"

These last words were starting to confuse them slightly. "The problem, where's the problem?" "Well I didn't get around to telling the others each time."

"They will just have to put up with it then, after all it's you choice not theirs." "Yeah ordinarily it would be, but I didn't get around to divorcing them either, none of them. I now have three wives and they have at last, all found out."

This cracked them up, there was Sid the quiet one, not thinking he had anything to add when hearing the others stories, had the best one of all.

The door opened and in walked Lula Belle, looking around she soon spotted Des. She was truly the most beautiful woman they had seen for a long time, you name it she had it. The three of them just gawked at her. "Come on Honey pot your mine again," she pouted. The accent added to her demeanour. "You never call me Honey pot Lula," said Harry. She just smiled that smile and walked him out.

Three left, whose next I wonder, the door opened again slowly as if the user was uncertain of the way. Sid slid down and under the table as her features revealed themselves. Whispering, "Its number one."
"Hi Sid, a word outside," she said. Sid moved out from under the table and escorted her out not wanting to cause a scene in front of his friends.

"Well that's the two womanisers gone, so we must be safe as I see it!!"

As they were thinking this the door burst open and there stood two burly Policemen. The remainder of them were rounded up and driven away.

There really were some good stories in that pub and I will never forget some of them. Things improved after that and my work picked up again, so it was good bye to the pub and nose back on the grind stone.

The plumbing job

I wasn't a qualified plumber, but my engineering experience led me into it as a plumbers mate. I could tackle most jobs except the boiler installations, for some reason these were kept for the qualified plumbers, of which I wasn't one.
This puzzled me a lot and much time was spent on it trying to get to grips with it.

In the past I had had all the plumbing experience thrust upon me one day as our old boiler needed to be changed. My work had dried up so I took charge of getting this thing priced up.

The first to visit was the salesman from the Gas board, he came in all full of the joys of spring and proceeded to scan my place. "What do you want me to price for?" Was his first comment. Explaining that what I needed were all the radiators replaced and a new condensing boiler. You have to accept that things are moving on in technology and not to buck the trend, but to go with it and move on, was my mode of thinking.

Chin rubbing time," I don't know if that's really what you want as the gas pipe has to be increased in size to accommodate a condensing boiler, you would have to have the kitchen floor up as well," he was trying to steer me up the wrong path already. "What you really need here is a conventional boiler. Straight out with the old one and in with a new, plus a stainless water tank is the way to go." Then proceeded to show me on his computer, in picture form what the new parts looked like. It really was child's stuff.

Now I must say that I don't like being talked down to, I really don't. He was really starting to piss me off what with the flash talk and the childish images on the screen. As if I didn't know what a radiator and a boiler looked like. I do after all have one stuck on my kitchen wall and radiators all around the house. Then the clever pricing started. "You will need one of these, that's so much extra and then this will be a bit more and so it went on." Just looking at him he had never done a real days work in his life. My back was up and he had only been in here about an hour. Then the shifty part started, “If you move you gas and electricity accounts back to us then there’s another reduction. How’s that? If you sign today I will throw in a free mag-cleaner!”

I’d had just about enough and refused his offer.

Now the next place was the large local plumbing firm recommended by a neighbour. So who turns up but a young guy covered with cement dust, old torn overalls and a piece of bent paper to write on. This is more like it, at last someone who knows his stuff, there wasn’t any refusing to install a condensing boiler and the radiators were measured and he was on his way in half an hour. “I will get an estimate to you in the post very soon.” These were the magic words you needed to hear and I had heard them.

Three weeks passed and nothing, so it was ring them up time. Full of apologies the manager pointed out that they were over their heads with work and promised to get it done that day, sure enough it was through the door that afternoon. Much cheaper than the Gas board it was the way to go. Accepting the price the next morning, I was surprised to be informed that they could start the work the very next week. They certainly knew how to move this lot.

We spent the weekend moving things in the kitchen and the furniture around to allow access to the radiators. Monday morning eight o'clock was to be the start time for an installation taking three days. Guess what? They didn't arrive, this dragged out until 4 o'clock in the afternoon then I rang the manager. "Didn't you get my message?" he said. "We didn't start yours today because when fitting new radiators you don't need your system cleaned out." I should have seen the writing on the wall at this point, I didn't.

The next day he did eventually turn up, the guy with torn overalls and cement dust. It was gone twelve, but he worked like mad and got the old boiler out and made good the wall. Were we on the way, I wondered?

The following day not a sign of him, then just as midday came so did he. We started to call him the

PM plumber, the only way we could survive it all was to make it fun and have a laugh.

Full of enthusiasm he gently stroked the now drying made good plaster. “That’s looking nice,” he declared. “Now what’s next, oh I need a couple of 15mm fittings and I’m away.” Disappearing out of the door with a. “Back in a few minutes!” Comment. We didn’t see him for three more days.

Oh what fun we thought, the weather was really warm so we amused ourselves until his untimely return. He did turn up and made some excuse about helping an old lady out and how he couldn’t just leave her stranded without hot water. We were very sympathetic, saying we understood perfectly his dilemma. Yeah Right! It wasn’t difficult to tell if he would be here tomorrow as he would take his tools with him when he wasn’t coming back the next day. I did say to him, “You’re not coming back tomorrow if you’re taking your tools with you.” His answer to that was that he had a private job to do that evening.

The next time we got two hours further work and he disappeared again, the next day turning up at midday, a few quick hours work. Then away again for a few more days, this time it was the suppliers that had sent the wrong boiler. He must have had six or seven jobs on the go at any one time so could only dilute the work between us all.

Looking at the economics of this it was plain to see that there wasn’t any money coming into the company as it was all out there in materials and unfinished work. Three weeks had passed by now and all we had was a new boiler installed and the old radiators still in situ with a replacement leaning against it.

Time to play some games of our own I thought. He rang up to say that he would be here tomorrow and get things moving. He did turn up or so he said, but we had a day out and missed him, oh dear what a shame. Promising to come the next day he said that his boss had told him to finish by the week-end. Guess what, we were out again.

His boss rang to say they needed to finish it and would we be there tomorrow. I assured him we would be, this he was pleased to hear and also his plumber Mr PM would be here bright and early. I know this will sound weird, but the next day we were called away to an old lady that needed her hot water sorting out, you know how it is.

His boss rang up and became very irate as he said that he needed to get things finished up very quickly and that his plumber had tried three times to finish the job, but couldn't get access and would we be good enough to be there tomorrow bright and early. I then had a meltdown saying that we didn't want the job finished this week as we had other things to do and could his man ring up sometime next week and arrange an appointment that he could manage to keep rather than one he couldn't.

You could hear him blowing a fuse. An hour later there was a knock on the door and there stood the manager. Now I've seen some big guys in my time, but this one was a giant, bellowing and used to getting his own way. He surely didn't understand that his approach to things was winding me up big-time. Having a very sinister side to me I let it out. After all I now held all the cards as they did a few weeks ago. Things had turned around, it was my turn to muck him about and I'm good at it.

"Now this is the situation," I said, "I don't want you to finish this until I'm ready and that won't be soon, maybe next week, or the week after, depends how I feel at the time. If you don't get it finished when I say. Then I have a plumber friend that will come in and complete the work for you. I will then deduct his charge from your bill, he's very expensive by the way!! He has been round and promises me that it will be two day's work at most." He changed in that very instant from the big blusterer to the-"Let's talk things through, I can see that you are upset at the way we did this and I apologise for any inconvenience you have suffered. How would it be if we left it until Monday morning and then start nice and early? Come on how would that suit you." Very calmly and quietly I explained that I would need longer than that to get over it and maybe if he had the kindness to allow me time to recover, do the decent thing and ring me next Thursday. I would by then have fully recovered and it gave him two days to get it done before the week-end.

He turned on his heels and disappeared. Fuming.

The phone did ring later the next week and they came round and finished it by the week-end. That you would think was the end of it, but oh no, the Gas safety certificate wasn't issued as Mr PM wasn't registered. The commissioning was carried out by another employee, he didn't submit the details, or leave me a copy of the safety certificate as they owed him money. I did manage to get it all passed off eventually. The manager to this day can't quite understand why I only paid part of the bill, I am not expecting a phone call anytime soon.

It was quite a good job and the money as a plumbers mate was sort of okay. I got on rather well with my mate Matthew, but I couldn't help thinking that I had met him somewhere before. We would do a few days here and a few days there trying to keep six or seven jobs on the go at the same time.

I asked him one day while we were having our lunch-break what other jobs had he done and was surprised to find out that he had been much like me. He would put up with it for a while and then move on much the same as I had. He would work on the fairgrounds in the summer and do the plumbing in the winter.

Then he told me of his time working in the local post office on the sweets and tobacco counter. This was just another infill job, but he said it was the best place for some good stories as there was always something going on.
Listen to this, he said, "My Granny would go in there on pension day and this is what she told me one day.

Did you know that there are spies that are sent around the post offices checking out the counter staff? They are not a patch on MI5, but all the same, just as shifty.

They are made up of a bunch of human beings that can only think of jobs worth, mingling with the regular customers and blending in, dressed up in civvies. You would need an experienced eye to realise just who they were.

These are highly trained individuals that would pass off as customer's any day of the week. Their training camp is somewhere on Salisbury plain cloaked in secrecy. These individuals are trained up to the hilt in all the latest surveillance techniques.

After six weeks of intensive training, they are let loose on the poor unsuspecting counter staff, who after all said and done are the salt of the earth as you well know. Helpful, with a welcoming smile in all weathers and useful advice on daily matters, including a few gardening tips picked up from a previous customer the day before. Along with the helpful questions, like how much is the value of your International package and then trying to encourage you to pay up for insurance that you don't really need. Pushing old ladies into recorded delivery and special delivery when ordinary first class would do. I ask you.

These special techniques are fostered on them at their monthly seminars, the idea is to boost the

Post Offices takings. There are targets to meet and the spies are there to make sure that these things are being pushed. Can you even believe that the Post Offices have a sales target to meet in the first place? It took me a while to get my head around that, but there it is.

So it came to pass that our local Post Office was targeted by these unsavoury individuals. The counter staff as I said had no idea that was the case until they got their monthly assessment, failing miserably. They were instructed to pull their socks up big time.

The pressure was on them the next day as the poor helpless patrons arrived, each one being grilled as to the contents contained within the package and the value? Granny was in the queue and overheard the old dear in front say to her friend that she hoped that they wouldn't ask as to the contents in her package. Granny by now was all ears as the queue shortened. Creeping closer to the worried lady in front, the moment was soon upon them. Granny at this point turned up her hearing aid volume to maximum "Could you tell me please what's inside?" The old lady froze totally unable to speak for a few moments.

The remainder of the queue were also onto it, one or two of them had also adjusted the volume on their hearing aids not wanting to miss anything. Straining to hear the answer, red faced she announced. "It's a vibrator." Well to say the place filled up with red faces was an understatement. (Granny by the way couldn't bring herself to mention the word vibrator when telling me this story, so she wrote it down on a piece of paper and passed it under the table.) The poor old counter staff all shared the embarrassment together.

Granny turned to her friend Hilda, "I wonder if it's the latest deluxe model, the three speed ribbed? Only they are hard to get and are only available on line, second hand." "I had no problem getting mine," replied Hilda. Still red faced the counter staff then asked if it contained batteries, to which the old lady replied, "Yes and a spare set as well."

I know you're dying to ask, did it get posted? Having ascertained that they weren't Lithium ion batteries, it was duly posted. The old lady left in a hurry looking at the floor. The moral of this story is, if you need to post a vibrator or your copy of Erotica weekly in the near future, just go somewhere they don't know you, or call it a Metronome."

He went on, a few weeks later this happened.

Granny told me of the lady in the queue that told her friend that her husband had just had a new catheter fitted. The hard of hearing friend misheard the word and thought it was carpet. The ensuing conversation was the best fun ever to overhear. The lady gradually realised that her friend hadn't quite got it when she mentioned how nice it would be to run a vacuum cleaner over it and what were they doing with the old one. It's a bugger this getting old thing.

Granny would often talk of the couple in the queue she met every Tuesday. (Pension day) He was the very smartest of all the men there, always immaculate, tie, suit and polished shoes. He never saw a mirror that didn't like him.

She was also extra special in her appearance, the one thing with these two is they would on occasion go for it big time. This would take the form of snide remarks followed by a few nasty insults. It was always over as fast as it started, but on occasion it was no holds barred as these two vented their steam.

This particular day there must have been words spoken on the way to the Post Office as they just concluded their previous set-to while still in the queue.

"So who's this Svetlana that you speak to on-line late at night and why do you need that Webcam?"
"She's just a friend that likes to show me things."
"Are you paying for something, come on tell me!"
With this he let go, "Well it's not much good asking you anymore, so I get my kicks on-line. As for paying, she is very reasonable and there isn't any chance of me catching anything, now is there!!

You only have to ask and she is very accommodating, which is more than we can say for you, isn't it. Svetlana is a memory maker, I think she's very sweet!"

"So you make a request and then its pay up time, is that how it works?"

"Yes that's exactly it, happy now?"

"One of these days the police will catch up with you by tracing that card back."

"I doubt that they ever will."

"Whys that?"

"Simple, I always use yours."

Granny felt sorry for the counter staff at Christmas as they were working all hours just trying to keep up without a break and they didn't even have time for a coffee, so Granny did the Boy Scout thing and took a flask of coffee and a small jar of sugar. Not at the time realising that it was the urine jar Grandad used on his visits to the doctors. The staff will probably end up with a verruca, swollen nuts, or worse.

We really did have some pleasant stories in the following months and my all-time favourite was the football story. Matthew had a way of telling it, it really had me hooked.

"It all started one cold winter's day. My wife who was an ardent football fan would catch the football bus each Saturday, with renewed anticipation of a win.
Me, well you know, I watched it on the TV and enjoyed it. Nice and warm, feet up, bottle of wine. While sitting there waiting to get the full experience I devised a plan to reduce my flavour blur. Cunningly crafting a small wooden seed tray type box, I then placed into it a square of turf cut from the middle of the front lawn, feet up on the beauty and suddenly things came to life, I had the lot.

The atmosphere, the smell of the pitch and the roar of the crowd. Cracked it in one. I was slowly becoming transfixed with that team as they approached the opponent's goal for the third time in an hour. My wife never knew that I watched the match every week on the box that was my little secret. These afternoons would pass in quiet isolation while the tempest flowed at the stadium.

As the level in the wine bottle dropped my enthusiasm for the game increased proportionally.

The home coming was the hardest part as I needed to act nonchalant, just casually asking her how things went, but knowing full well the score and the pain she suffered on most occasions.

The dog suddenly made a bolt for the back of the settee as the front door squeaked open. The wife had eventually made it back home after the bus had broken down again for the third time this month. Visibly perturbed by her experience she dragged herself in, battered and down at mouth not really wanting to discuss anything in the first few minutes. “How did your team do then?” The long face gave me the inevitable answer. “We lost two-nil.”
“What against that lot I don’t believe it.”

So it was, we were waiting again for the future pleasure than only a win can convey.

The next Monday morning I had an appointment at the local Doctors surgery. The usual thing greeted me as I entered, it was full of and you guessed it, local football supporters all

wanting some reassurance that things would change. Some in heated discussion about the match and others that had succumbed to lethargy just lolling around holding the walls up.
A pitiful sight it really was, but there again this was happening on a regular basis. The Doctors had by now sharpened up their act by instructing the receptionist to check the football results every Sunday, so if need be they could be ready Monday morning for the onslaught.

"Okay lads be upstanding," shouted the Doctor, accompanied by the duty nurse who was carrying the medication for such events on a very large tray. The surgery staff called it their Monday tray, it was always left fully loaded and stored in the side cupboard. That's called forward planning. They knew the drill from last time and the times before. Forming up in a line the doctor then administered the antidote. Passing along the line each was given a choice of an enema, or half a glass of Whisky. "Top or bottom?" She enquired as she passed along the queue.
Most knew the difference and chose the drink, but Sten was really down and went for both, as he

said he needed a fresh start all round. Fan number nine in the row, you know the one, the one sporting that silly looking lime coloured fluorescent away kit, asked a silly question.
“Will this treatment make things better Doctor?”
“No, no you silly man, nothing will ever make it better and you should know that by now.”
By the time she had reached the end of the queue the fans that had been treated earlier were starting to giggle and things were very slowly returning to normality, much to the surprise of those still waiting to be treated.

One or two of them had removed their team colours and now felt able to re-adorn themselves. Silly nonsense, I heard myself mutter more than once, it was at last my turn to get some treatment for my conjunctivitis. Eye strain from watching too much TV if you must know.
Buying some fertiliser for my turf square on the way home, I was more than ready for the next game.

New horizons

I bumbled along for a few more years struggling to keep myself afloat. The work was intermittent to say the least. It was at last time to try something else while I was still out of debt. The cement factory was just across the river from where we lived and within walking distance and paid good wages.

The first morning there I was supplied with high visibility overalls and a hardhat, something that I had overlooked in my past life, in engineering there wasn't the need for such things. I was walked across the yard and was introduced to Tony Wynyard the foreman of the gypsum mill. Here was the biggest man I had ever seen, he was like a giant, big hands and an even larger hardhat perched on top of his head.

My first site of the gypsum mill filled me with trepidation. First the crushing mill and those massive turning rollers, then onto a ball mill which was the size of our house, it consisted of a massive rotating circular barrel filled with iron shot the size of cannon balls. As the barrel turned the iron shot pummelled the gypsum into fine dust. Nothing came out of that barrel larger than a grain of sand.

I gradually got used to the noise and the sheer confusion of this place and began to fall into the rhythm of the job. It was easy to understand, the gypsum was first smashed up in the mill by those massive rollers and then loaded into the ball mill, where it was finally processed into fine powder.

Occasionally Tony and Simon the van driver would put a large bag of something else in with it. I asked the two lads I worked with Dermot and Patrick what they thought it was, but they had no idea any more than I did. It was delivered in a red van every few days or so. None of it added up, why put that sack of stuff in there every so often and it seemed to always be done just at dinnertime when we were going for our one hour lunch break. Most people would have ignored such things, but I have always had an inquisitive nature and wanted to understand why?

I was determined to find out the answer to all of this and kept my eye out for that red van for the next few days. Sure enough on the eighth day it appeared once again and parked up over the back of the car park concealed behind some storage sheds. Right I thought to myself, today we will find out the answer one way or other.
It wasn't a difficult place to conceal oneself, what with the machinery and believe it or not, you could actually hide behind the noise, as it takes away the senses. I had by now crept up as near as possible to the mill and waited patiently partly concealed by a storage rack.

The red van reversed slowly in until it was as near as it could get it to the mill. The driver who was unknown to me beckoned Tony over. On opening the back doors I could see what I thought were sacks but were in fact body bags.
The two of them struggled to get the first one into the mill hopper and I watched it slowly being consumed by those rollers. They had considerable difficulty with the second one as whoever it was in there was still alive and kicked out as if putting up a final struggle. This one was also consumed by

the rollers, but not before I heard those terrifying screams just as they disappeared into the jaws of this mighty machine.

The business was done, Tony and the driver quickly jumped into the van and sped away. It was all over in a split second, but I had seen it. I waited at least ten minutes to make sure the coast was clear before creeping over towards that belching monster spewing out its deadly secret.

The contents of the hopper had by now fed into the machine and were on their way up the conveyor belt towards the ball mill opening. The only remaining clue to what went on was a piece of blood soaked cloth snagged in the hopper. This I quickly concealed in my pocket. It was over for whoever it was and I wished them peace.

Sleep wasn't my friend that night. I had seen things that were not of my doing, private things, with private meanings.

All to do with others and not for my eyes, or my understanding. I puzzled at some of it, why in the gypsum mill of all places, not exactly private, but deadly permanent. Why not somewhere else more remote? Well perhaps we will find the answer to that one day.

The next morning Dermot appeared to be very worried. “Patrick walked out yesterday dinner time and hadn’t been seen since.”
“Well Dermot what do you expect with a job like this, I have felt like doing it more than once and I’ve only been here a few weeks.”

The day progressed and there wasn’t any sign of Patrick. Tony walked past me a few times and cut me a look, what for, how would I know?

It was no good, whenever I got this way with work there was only one thing for it and that was to jack the bloody thing in and finish it off forever. So with this I collected up my stuff and headed for the door.

I bade farewell to Dermot and told him not to worry too much about Patrick as he had probably gone up the pub and was sleeping it off somewhere.

I left that night carrying all my things, on the way out I offered Tony the finger and parted company with them forever, vowing never to return. It was time to move on once again. I had done it again and found myself unemployed. Not for the first time in my life I was once again looking for work.

Time for something different

I had earned good money at the cement works and had by now saved enough to carry me through for a few weeks hoping my self-employed business would pick up again in the meantime. There were many considerations as to what sort of work to search for. I really wanted something a bit different from those mucky jobs with good money, maybe it was time to venture forward into a more sophisticated job, what, I didn't know.

Not much happened around our street, it was unusually quiet the day the door knocked too loudly for my liking. The kind of knock that demands attention.

My fat friend

On opening the door there stood the fat lady from over the back. Now I didn't like this woman at all and I mean, at all. There was something about that overly fat face peering back at me that gave me the jitters, she was short in stature and was as wide as she was tall, in engineering terms she would be described as over square by a long way.

From what was only a few years ago a quite an attractive woman, or so I had heard. “Your tree has just knocked my hat off, what are you going to do about it then!!” Now you may or you may not know that I have an inbuilt sinister streak and I know it. “We could go and tell the tree off big time how’s that, or perhaps I could help you back on with your hat.” She looked at me with disdain and was not amused, but there again she couldn’t be amused at any time, even if she tried.
That was the nature of the beast. My Silver birch tree was an absolute beauty and really did grace the street. Along the side of the fence it was overhanging the pavement by a fair amount of that there was no discussion, it did.

Some of the lower branches were such that you would indeed need to duck as you passed. The thing here was that to remove these branches the whole shape of the tree would be compromised giving it a lop–sided look. That’s the reason I held on for as long as I had, before doing the deed.

Across the road from us there was a family that had at least three young boys with a lot more energy than their little bodies could handle. They were engaged to do the honours under strict supervision, I knew what young lads were like when they have a chance to destroy something they get carried away and very quickly.

"Right boys that branch there, that one and that one there to start with, pointing to the offending branches, then we will look at it and move on if necessary. They tore into things at a pace, each one trying to outdo his brothers and they were really out of control as I thought they would be. "Whoa lads, time to consider." Standing back and reviewing the situation, there was only two more branches to come off before the job was finished. I engaged them in the consideration part of this by saying what do you think? The easiest way was for them to agree to be careful and lead them slowly into the responsibility of it all. The tree by now had lost its shape, there was nothing for it, but to be reasonable and to that woman of all people and it was very hard to swallow.

The boys had sawn the branches off and then the next thing was to drag them through the house and up to the end of the back garden. Where their fun really was to start. A fire was lit with a rush to get it all going, smoke rising and I must admit on a very breezy day it was going everywhere.

Now you could call me complicated in the mind, or just pissed off, but the motion of the smoke was to me my last concern as I was totally under protest at doing this in the first place, being more aggravated by the messenger, than the task itself.

The boys then told me when I eventually returned that the woman over the back fence had complained that the smoke was filling her bedrooms. "Have you got it yet Boys? This is the same woman that complained about the overhanging tree in the first place, I will have you know!!"

I knew that I was blowing steam this morning, but I was beyond consideration for anyone at this point. The faggot complained about the overhanging branches and then complains about the smoke from the resulting fire, well I never. I was chewing broken glass by now.

A few weeks later I met Dermot in the pub, he said that Patrick hadn't returned to work and seemed very upset that he just left without any reason. So to cheer him up I told him the story including the following update.

"I was in the back garden minding my own business; then I'm afraid it all happened very quickly. That woman's cat frequented my garden and spent a lot of time digging up my much loved flower borders. It had suddenly appeared lurking in the undergrowth on a mission to catch another bird, which it would just kill and leave there decaying.

You might say that it is only natural for a cat to do this and I would agree, but it was only natural for my dog to try and tear the arse out of the cat as well, wouldn't you say. It is also natural for someone like me that gets pissed off with cats killing birds, to put up with it. Having racing pigeons when I was a lad and having to fight the cats off, I was well rehearsed in what to do in these circumstances.

It had by now caught a full sized wood Pidgeon. The fight was on to save it and I meant it, snapping into action speed was of the essence and I had to get to that Pidgeon before the cat had a second bite, the first bite for the cat was usually a mouthful of feathers.

Grabbing the cat's throat from behind and increasing the pressure on its neck while at the same time gently supporting the Pidgeon was the only to go. This had to be executed at arm's length to keep away from those claws. With the cat dangling from my grip. Sometimes a quick process, on others a long drawn out contest, but always successful.

At this very moment the face appeared over the fence. Those peering little eyes staring out from the fat roundel of a face greeted me as I performed this most delicate task, I must admit I was glad it was her cat as I choked the dear life out of it watched by the loving owner

That fat faggot really needed to abdicate from that chocolate and fast. “What are you doing to my cat?” she yelled.
“About the same as your cat is doing to my Pidgeon!” Was all I could think of and then the silly nonsense really did start, what with the screaming and the insults. The words murder and cruel sod where ever present as this rather unusual contest unfolded. I waited patiently for the glorious outcome.

In the end the instinct of the cat waned as it fought for its last breathe and the contest was over. The feeling that you get when the pigeon flies off is always worth it.

She never spoke to me again and I often thought that it was unfortunate that these things came together all at once. The cat did return to my garden after a short absence and continued its hunting skills on my garden wildlife, but it would always cock me a side kite as it passed.

Bob finally arrives

This job was the only one available after my sudden departure from the cement factory. I had really tried to get gainful employment for many weeks, but to no avail, everything failed, as one application after another was turned down. Then the Mortuary assistant's job cropped up. The job itself was just about the most unpleasant undertaking that was possible to imagine, but the money was good.

The door burst open and to my great relief my pal Bob had arrived at last to save the day. "You okay Jim, sorry I'm late, another problem with the trains this morning as usual, how far have you got?"
"That's the wrong way to do it, you have to start at the upper rib cage and draw down like this gesturing with his hand the general direction to go. One more thing have you checked the body ID only I think that that's the wrong one! She came in yesterday afternoon, the one we want is number twenty two the next one along. What have I said

about double checking every time?" With this comment Bob lifted the covering from her face and it was then that I recognised her from a few years ago.

I didn't know quite what to do, was I to declare a conflict of interest, or maybe keep quiet. There was only one thing for it and that was to be up front. "I know her she used to live up the road from me, her name is Moira. We dated one night, it was going fine until I upset her on the way home and that was that so to speak."
"We've got time, tell me the story."
"Well it was like this Bob.

I was just fourteen and three quarters at the time, my main interests were Motor cycles and doing anything greasy. Girls were just not on my agenda at all. A few doors up the street was the house where Moira lived.

Moira was nearly sixteen and had a crush on me for the last few months. I would see her coming and make for the front door, most times I was successful in my endeavours. This time I failed as she crept up behind him, "Hello handsome, you're looking good, how about you take me out sometime?"

The last thing I wanted was to be seen walking along with a girl, it would be too much, perhaps my friends would notice and call me names. On this day for some reason it didn't seem such a silly idea, she was pretty. "Where would you like to go? How about the fairground, this evening eight o'clock."

"I will look forward to it!" Well that was it then date made. I tidied myself up, Moira was ready on time and the pair of us set off for the fair. It was just getting dark so I relaxed as we strolled along the river. "Would you like to hold my hand Jim?" I looked around, the coast was clear, none of my mates were fishing.

"Only along this part, go on then." Strolling along hand in hand, I thought to myself, it's not so bad after all this hand holding. "How about a kiss then handsome."

"Just a quick one then, that's all." Things were moving on a pace I thought, she will want to marry me before we get to the fair. All sorts of things were going through my head as we turned into the field.

These thoughts were soon forgotten as we drew closer, the noise the music, the shouts and the screams soon blinded any thoughts I had. First the Dodgems, giving me the chance to show off my driving skills. Then the rocket and the rest in turn were all tried out. We both had a great time trying the rides out. Towards the end of the evening with both of us dizzy from our experiences, the last thing to do was to buy a couple of Candy Flosses for the trip home.

Well this is the point where it all started to unravel. I reached for my money only to find enough to buy one. “Fancy sharing one between us?”
“Yes why not?” Walking back along the river we stopped every now and then for a bite each. After a while there wasn’t much left as we turned towards each other sharing the last few bites. “One for you and then one for me,” she joked. Her grip on the stick tightened with each remaining bite. I looked into her big brown eyes, there was a sinister glint that at first I hadn’t noticed, but as

the floss got smaller this look became more intense. I was reading her thoughts as to what she was up to.

At last we faced each other for the final bite and then I twigged onto her little game. “Who’s going first?” I said.
“I will,” came back the quick reply. I was ready as she bent forward to take her last bite, I then stubbed the last remaining floss into her face.

Well to say that was the end of the hand holding was an understatement she never spoke to me again.

Years later as a guest at a friend’s wedding I met her again. At the buffet later I asked her if I could get her a sandwich, or something else to eat. “Maybe you would prefer a candy floss instead!” I said wondering whether she would still remember. We both laughed at this and she admitted that it was her intention to do the very same. “You just beat me to it Jim!”

Bob was taken with the story and the way I told it. “What else did you get up to when you were a kid?”

"What didn't we get up to would be a better question!" He seemed interested in what I had to say and well I do like to chat on about things so I offered him the interesting parts of my life story along with a few stories passed on by others, on a plate. We sat there next to Moira drinking a cup of tea and I began. I had only been going for a few minutes when there was a knock on the door and a head peered in. "I've come for the body that's going to the hospital Bob." It was none other than Simon the red van driver.

"Can you put this one back together Jim, just throw all the organs back inside and put it into a body bag while I talk to Simon?" Well there I was stumped not knowing what to do. I started to think about things and decided that she wasn't going anywhere while I had a choice. I tidied Moira up and changed her ID for number twenty two.

I was curious as to just who the other body was before I let it go into the van and off to the gypsum mill. Slowly pulling the zip down I was in total shock to see Patrick laying there. I couldn't help thinking that he didn't look dead, but was just asleep. I felt his face and he was definitely still warm. Shit I thought now what? There was only one thing left for it and I acted fast, racing across the room I hit the emergency fire alarm button.

Bob and Simon came rushing back in wondering what the hell had happened. "What's going on Jim?"
"Search me the thing just went off on its own as far as I know." The distant wailing of the fire engines could be heard miles away as they came closer and closer. Bob and Simon started to panic and quickly wheeled number twenty two out and placed it into the van. With this Simon drove quickly out of the gates and disappeared. It wasn't long after that the fire engines arrived and all hell broke loose as they swarmed into the building looking for the fire. Followed a short time later by the police.

I informed the police of my findings expecting them to throw themselves into action, but no not a bit of it. They treated it as some form of intrusion into their work and would I stop interrupting their investigation. I tried to explain that time was of the essence and they needed to move quickly before Patrick arrived at the gypsum mill. Alas it all fell on deaf ears. There was only one thing for it and that was to ring Dermot and explain to him what was going on at the cement works.

I prayed that he was near his phone and had stopped work for his lunch break as he did have a habit of working through to get the last load finished before breaking off.

The phone rang and rang with a desperate sounding tone, but still no answer. Where the bloody hell is he, it seemed like an age before a voice in broken English answered. “Stop the mill working Dermot, they have Patrick in the van and he will the next one to go in and that will be the end of him.”
“I no understand you Jim, go in where?”
“Those sacks that they put in the gypsum mill are body bags, the next one to arrive has Patrick inside it, understand?”
“I don’t know how to stop the mill, leave it up to me I will think of something.” With that I left it up to Dermot, but I was still worried that he hadn’t fully understood the seriousness of the situation.

It was time to try to re-engage with the police, who by now had settled down and where starting to listen to me at last. “I used to work at the cement factory down by the river and while there I saw some strange things going on. They were dumping bodies into the gypsum crusher and they have just taken one from here that was still alive. You need to act very quickly and stop them before it’s too late.”

Bob came sidling over wondering what the fuss was all about. On getting the gist of my conversation with the police he informed the officers that I was the new boy and had got my wires crossed. “Jim is new to all of this and is employed on work experience, just a few weeks on trial you understand. We do at times take on those with employment issues and he is one of them.” It was no good even trying after that, Bob had finished any consideration that the police had for my information and they brushed me aside.

Emergency

I just stood there not knowing what to do as this thing had by now crashed down around my ears. Bob wasn't talking to me for obvious reasons, the police discounted anything that I said as rambling. My thoughts were for my good friend Patrick who at this minute was being transported to the gypsum mill and his certain end. The fire brigade had finished their enquiries and had departed. The police on the other hand were still listening to Bob and his farfetched story of events.

There was nothing I could do although I didn't stop thinking about things. The cement factory was too far away for me to get there in time, I was relying on Dermot to work some magic. I didn't have to wait long as my phone was ringing its head off as I entered the rest-room. It was one of those once in a lifetime moments when I anticipated good news and it arrived as expected.

A shaking little voice in broken English full of fear and squeaking in hushed tones said. "Is that

you Jim, Dermot here? I have big problems, I won't be working for the cement factory ever again when they find out what I've done."
"What have you done, come on Dermot what was it? "
"I pinched the van, it reminded me of when we smuggled ourselves across the channel all of those years ago and arrived in your pleasant country. I hotwired the ignition and I am parked round the back of the Mortuary right at this moment with Patrick still inside, how's that old buddy? Did I get that one right or what?"

"You little beauty, dead on Dermot you couldn't have done better." I then raced round to the back door and greeted an over excited Dermot with the largest grin on his face that I had ever seen. He had already unzipped the body bag to give Patrick some air. I checked his pulse and it was still going strong, but he looked as if he was still well out of it for some reason. "Get that engine started up we need to get Patrick straight to hospital. Dermot drove like fury guided by my directions while I attended to Patrick in the back of the van.

I could see the funny side of things as Patrick and I were thrown around inside the back of the van while Dermot made siren noises to add to the situation. It started to dawn on me that Dermot just couldn't drive at all as he was rattling through the gears in some sort of random way as he had seen it done on the television. The gears were crashing and the van suddenly slowed down for no good reason as the wrong gear had been selected and thrust into unnecessary action.

We arrived at the hospital in a shower of smoke and dust. "I can't go in there Jim, there's something I forgot to tell you. We are on the run as we are failed asylum seekers and have been ordered to go back. We just skipped bail and moved on to this part of the country. If I go in there then they will ask me my name and that would be the end of it for me and Patrick."

It was time for some quick thinking and at last it occurred to me that the only way was to brazen it out and say as little as possible. Between us we managed to drag Patrick into the Accident and Emergency department and laid him out on the floor in front of the reception desk. I told Dermot to say nothing and play the deaf mute in case they twigged that he wasn't from this part of the world.

The nurse looked shocked and her first question was. "What happened to your friend?" "He got mixed up in things that were nothing to do with him, a case of mistaken identity." As she filled in the form she asked. "What's his name?"
"Patrick O'Leary from Dublin," she just looked at me and you could see that she wasn't going to believe that one, but she just wrote it down and moved on, the moment had passed. "Why is he in a body bag?" she asked. "That's all we had at the time to keep him warm."

Dermot and I were relieved when they took him away and started to treat him. The two of us waited patiently in the waiting room with the other anxious relatives waiting for news. "Do you think they believe he is an Irishman Jim?" Dermot whispered.
"Bloody no chance, there aren't many black Irishmen called Patrick O'Leary now are there? That's not the way it works over here Dermot, these people will look after Patrick very well regardless of his identity. I do have one question

though, how did you two come to have names like Dermot and Patrick when the chances of that in real life are just about zero"

We just sat in the waiting room and Dermot opened up on his past life. "Patrick and I both lived in the same village in Somalia. We were very poor and things as you know have fallen apart in our country. There was a war going on and piracy. Well the day came when we heard about a couple of other boys from the village that had made it all the way to Britain and we decided to have a try ourselves, well why not we thought, perhaps we can make it too. The first part of our journey was the easiest as we stole a car and made it to the border with Kenya. Ending up in Mombasa docks, here we smuggled ourselves aboard a ship, we didn't know where it was going until it reached Athens. When we got there we just joined in with all the other refugees going to Germany.

It was while we were in Athens that we started to drink in Paddy's Bar in the old part of town. Mohamed said that we needed to adopt English sounding names, the barmen had name tags on their shirts so we just pinched those. Mohamed became Patrick and I changed my name from Abdul to Dermot. The barmen taught us English and three months later there we were all of a sudden looking and sounding like English gentlemen. Some of our Somali friends said that the Irish don't speak proper English and we were learning it all wrong. We told them they were wrong to be sure, we're no eejits, the suns splitting the stones for us."

"I must admit at this point I nearly pissed myself laughing as here were two black Somalis calling each other by Irish names with Irish accents. Go on Dermot, where did you go after that?

"Well Jim the next part of our journey was the hardest as we had to walk and blend in with rest of those traveling to Germany. We then found out that there was a place in Calais where they had a refugee camp called the Jungle. So we headed there and from there we managed to walk through the channel tunnel and out the other side.

The police arrested us straight away as we didn't fit in and stood our sore thumbs out like, as you say over here. Patrick says it was more like fishes out of water, whatever that means."

The nurse then came in and said that we could visit Patrick as long as we didn't stay too long. She led us up to the ward and there propped up in bed was Patrick looking a lot better. Patrick tried to speak, but his words where jumbled. He did at last manage to convey that he knew what was going on and it was serious.

I knew I wouldn't get the rest of this story until Patrick had recovered. Dermot came back home with me after I found out that they were sleeping in a builders shed up on the new tower block construction site.

A few more days passed before we were allowed to visit Patrick and we both made our way there in anticipation of bringing this thing to a close. Patrick had recovered well enough to tell us of the journey he had made in the days that he was missing. "I got fed up working in the cement factory and decided to have a drink in the local pub and maybe return to work later that day. There was a poker game going on so I decided to chance my luck on the cards. We played it a lot back home and I was pretty good at it and knew how to cheat without the rest of them knowing.

I was doing well and winning before one of them sussed me out and that was that. A fight broke out and the next thing I knew I was tied up in some kind of building. These are dangerous people and not to be trifled with. The next morning they came into see me and spoke to me in my own language. They were very nice to me apologising for any inconvenience and would I like to do them a favour to justify my release.

I asked them just what it was they wanted and they told me I was to catch a plane back home to deliver a package, they explained that I was the only one that could do it as I spoke Somali Arabic. I told them that if I did it then the authorities would arrest me and never let me return.

They weren't very happy with my refusal and injected something into my arm, I then woke up here in hospital." Dermot and I just looked at each other. "That means Dermot, that Bob and the Mortuary are all linked in some way along with big

Tony and Simon. You don't suppose that they use the Mortuary as a clearinghouse for their unwanted victims and people that get in their way do you?"

As we left the hospital I told Dermot about Moira and my fear that she would end up in the gypsum mill. He was more than happy to help me get her out of there. So we devised a rescue plan that we would carry out this evening under the cover of darkness.

The van was hidden down at the bottom of our street and we waited until the clock struck twelve before loading up and making our way slowly so as not to attract too much attention. Parking up behind the Mortuary it all seemed a little strange to be back there, but with other purposes in mind. Dermot insisted that I let him have a go at the push button entry door lock before we forced the door. It seemed like an age while he fiddled with the push button combinations. A sudden click had the mechanism released, the door swung open, we were in.

Dermot at this point hesitated, he had smelt that smell of death many times before. “I’m okay now Jim, it just caught me by surprise that’s all!” he whispered. Now I thought as we approached the chiller drawers, what number did I change her for? It was all lost on me at that moment, there was only one way to do this and that was to unzip them all one at a time and do a visual inspection. Feeling our way about in the darkness in this very spooky place was starting to get to us.

A pair of car headlights suddenly flashed past illuminating the widows, we both dived for cover under the corpse dressing tables. The sound of the main doors opening and a van reversing.in concentrated our attention. The two voices were known to me as Simon and Bob’s. Two bodies were then quickly unloaded and placed on the table just above our heads. They then started to laugh about something that had occurred. The doors were locked up and they left just as the phone rang in the office. For some reason Bob decided to hurriedly return.

He answered it in English and then changed into Arabic as the conversation progressed. “What’s he

saying Dermot?" I whispered. "Shush," he said as he crept under the tables towards the office door trying to get a better understanding of the conversation. They chatted on for a while, Bob left soon afterwards locking the door behind him. We both gave a sigh of relief as things once again settled down. Creeping out from our hiding places the first thing I said was. "Come on, what was that all about?"
"Don't ask, we need to get this thing moving and fast, what does Moira look like?"
"Blue eyes blonde hair." We searched the place high and low. A short time later Dermot found her.
"Here we go Jim, this one, yes?"
"Yes, well done." It had taken some time to locate Moira and we eventually carried her out and placed her gently into the van. Dermot then headed straight back to the office and spent some time searching through the desk drawers and files. He quickly returned with a box folder. I checked that we had everything we had come with, while Dermot secured the rear door.

It wasn't without a certain amount of fear that we had at last managed it. The slow drive down the high street was punctuated by silence as we breathed a sigh of relief. It was then onto the backstreets, it was when we were winding our way home that I decided to bring up the subject of the telephone conversation.

Dermot held back for a while as he wrestled with the gears. "We have big problems Jim, they are kidnappers and hold people to ransom. Any that don't pay up are killed and processed through the Mortuary.

It's just about the last place the police would look for a body. Bob is married to Tony's daughter and he is one of the gang members. We also have another problem and that is they know where Patrick is so we will have to get him out of that hospital. They are going for him tomorrow night."

"Well done Dermot, what we need to do first is give Moira a decent burial. I thought up in the woods along by the river.

When we have that out of the way, then we will rescue Patrick. After that I have a little business proposal for you." We dug Moira a lovely grave overlooking the river and said a few prayers.

Dermot muttered a few words in Arabic which he said afterwards would ensure that she went to heaven. We did eventually get home that night after we hid the van behind some trees at the bottom of our street.

Kidnap incorporated

We had to be very careful what we did in the next few days as Bob and the others knew the whereabouts of Patrick and some of our involvement. Dermot thumbed through the files finally giving up. “Hey Jim can you read this stuff for me as Paddy’s bar was a little short on the written word.” Looking through the files we had just about everything we needed to finish these people off for good. There were complete records of the deceased and when they were disposed of, along with dates and other information appertaining to their situation. Phone numbers and the amount of ransom demanded. Followed by the letters C/F and the word “Divided.”
I pondered on these initials for a while and finally decided it must mean the cement factory, as for divided I had no idea at all.

It was without further discussion that Dermot turned the tables on me after seeing a list of names and phone numbers in the files. He phoned Bob threatening to tell police everything unless they pay up some money. This was typical of Dermot to act first and think about it afterwards. I wasn't too happy with this sudden freelance approach as we hadn't at this stage rescued Patrick.

Someone had to bring this little lot down to earth and get some organisation into it, or things would go haywire. We needed to plan events that involved Patrick.

"Right then Dermot, I have worked it all out, we will rescue Patrick this afternoon during visiting time. My plan is that we catch the bus to the hospital leaving the van concealed for the moment, why ask for trouble? When we get there we go for a stroll in the gardens and then leg it over the back wall before anyone notices. You okay with that?"
"It sounds a plan to be sure."

The bus trip had us both looking behind us most of the time as we weren't aware at this stage if they were on to us. Slipping into the hospital through a side door we made our way up to the ward expecting to see our friend all well and smiling. That wasn't the way it was going to work out for us. Patrick's bed was empty. The duty nurse informed us that he had gone for walk with his friends earlier. His side locker was empty which told us he wasn't coming back.

"They've got him Dermot, now what do we do? It might have been a better idea if you hadn't threatened them this morning."
"No problem Jim that's easy to rectify, we just go and get one of theirs and do the same to them, then we do a trade, that's how it works and always has." I could see that things were going in the wrong direction for me.
I was always the quiet person letting these things just happen. Dermot on the other hand had different ideas as he had been brought up with these things going on all around him for years.

"I have formulated a plan and I think you will like it Jim, when does Bob take his lunch break and where does he go?"
"Twelve thirty on the dot he locks up and goes to the Red lion pub in the high street, returning at one thirty precisely every day regular as clock work.

You must be bloody mad, we would never get away with it in broad daylight."
"You won't be getting away with anything as you're not going, this is a job for me and some of my mates. They owe me a few favours and are keen to pay them back, that's the way we work. I will need the van and you will need to stay here and guard the house just in case they try something on with you."

I was completely taken aback at these comments as this sort of thing I thought happened to everyone else and not to some unemployed guy looking for casual work. It would really start a war of some kind, each of us kidnapping the others and there wasn't as far as I could see any way out of it ending once it had started.

Dermot could see my worried look and tried to console me. "Don't worry Jim this is just normal, they won't even be annoyed that we turned the tables on them, they will just try to out manoeuvre us and think of something else to even the score up in the future, but they won't get it."
"Sod you and you're plans Dermot, I can see this little lot going tits up and very quickly, we are

getting into something deep and I for one would like to bail out while I can."
"You forget what they did to Moira?" I thought on and he was right they didn't treat her very well and maybe it was time to get even.

The day soon arrived after a sleepless night worrying how this was all to pan out. Dermot made a few phone calls before leaving to get the van. I was relieved not to be going with him as the whole lot of it filled me with dread.

Dermot and the van disappeared up the street and we were on for the biggest thing in our lives and the risks that go with them.

The street outside was very quiet and I was aware of the problems, they could bolster their position by kidnapping me as an extra pawn in their game. A slight tapping on the door had me frozen on full alert, was this the way it would happen? The postman hadn't been yet so maybe it was him, or perhaps the wind. Suddenly there it was again a gentle tap followed by another and then another. I wasn't going to fall for it as I crept up behind the curtains for a squinty.

There was someone there alright and at last they decided to leave and head on up the street. It turned out to be old Mrs Jones from the corner shop delivering my weekly magazine.

I breathed a sigh of relief and flopped back down in the chair, this thing wasn't even off the ground yet and my life had changed in an instant. The phone rang, I just stood there frightened to answer it.

Were they just checking that I was at home so they could come and get me? The next person to knock the door was the postman. I could see his red Post Office jacket through the glass panels. There was something to sign for and while I attended to my signature I glanced across the street to where there was a parked car that had two occupants observing my property. On seeing me looking they suddenly busied themselves with unnecessary talk and began to tidy the inside of the car up.

Perhaps things were starting to get to me, I knew they would sooner or later. Everyone that walked along the street was taking an interest in

the front of our house.
Two or three hours had passed by now, but no sign of Dermot. Had things gone badly, or was he on his way. It was about then that the penny dropped, what did he think he was going to do with Bob if he managed to kidnap him?

He would be bringing him back here I suppose, that was something else I hadn't reckoned on. It was about another half an hour before the van pulled up outside and a smiling Dermot showed his face. We have a surprise for you Jim, look who we have here?" Patrick's head popped out of the passenger door. "We found him in Bob's office tied up."
"So where's Bob?"
"He's in the back of the van tied up as well, there's just one thing I have to tell you Jim. Things didn't go quite go to plan."

The two of us lifted Bob from the back of the van and into our front room, the place we reserve for guests. "Bob's quiet Dermot what's wrong with him?"

"He's dead, we had a little accident as he resisted arrest, I fell on top of him and in doing so he cracked his head open on the pavement."
"What the hell is going on this wasn't part of the plan, tell me Dermot what are we going to do with him?"
"I thought we could take him down along the river and bury him next to Moira."

All the while we were talking about things Patrick had been busy in my drinks cabinet. He didn't seem to have suffered too badly from his ordeal.

When he had satisfied his needs Patrick came up with an idea. "We're going back to the cement mill to dispose of the body the way they liked to do it! And we will do it tonight."

It was just at this moment the door knocked rather loudly. "Who the bloody hell is that someone shouted?" I took another squinty through the curtains. "Whoever it is they are wearing a uniform, quick get Bob untied and sat up in the chair. Bob was propped up and given a newspaper to occupy himself.

I slowly and casually opened the door to find the electricity meter reader standing there. We let him in, on his return he commented. ”Having party boys?” He then looked at Bob reading the upside down newspaper. “Don’t give him anymore he looks too far gone!” We all agreed.

The end game

The plan was that after dark we would get the van parked outside and take Bob on his last trip in this world, the very way he had organised it for so many others. Dermot rustled up a bunch of flowers from somewhere, we folded his arms and placed the posy on his chest, we were ready to go at last. It would have to be the back streets until we reached the main road and the short trip to the cement factory.

On reaching the factory our first problem was the lights were on and there were people working there. We parked up along the road a short way and considered our next move. Patrick looked at us.
"They're not working at this time of night, no chance, there must be something going on for them to still be here.
"The gypsum crusher is going flat out judging by the noise," said Dermot. On further observation it looked from where we were that there were two of them loading up the crusher. Patrick decided to

take a closer look and returned a while later with information we didn't want to hear.

"Big Tony and Simon are putting bodies into the crusher and they have more than one in that truck, it takes at least five minutes to get rid of one. How about we give them another one they weren't expecting, wait a little while, then call the police and see how they talk their way out of it?"

We all chuckled at this as it was just about the best thing ever and we of course would have a ringside seat. Bob was still laid out in the back of the van, but said nothing. Dermot and Patrick insisted they do it all alone as they felt responsible in some ways for the others that went before them. This I couldn't figure out as they were not involved, so how do the feel any guilt I wondered.

Patrick and Dermot were going to love this little escapade and moved quietly round to the back of the van, they then slid Bob out and disappeared into the darkness. Everything went quiet, it was about five minutes later that their silhouettes appeared in the light emanating from the open factory door. They were carrying Bob on his last

journey.
He was soon in the truck and they sneaked back unnoticed. “Right that’s all done, now which of us should do the honours and call the police?” said Patrick. I had to step in here. ”It’s no good you two doing it with your Irish accents, they will soon know who you are, this is a job for a proper English gentleman, something you two aint.

“Hello is that the police station by any chance? We have a situation here that’s actually ongoing, there seems to be a break-in at the cement factory across the road from us and I thought maybe you could come and have a look?” Nothing happened for about five minutes then we heard the sirens in the distance.
It wasn’t long after that the flashing lights appeared. There was a certain amount of panic as those police cars squealed to a halt the yard.

Big Tony knew the game was up and just froze. Simon rushed over to close the trucks back door, at this point he must have seen Bob perched up in the back of it clutching a posy of flowers.

Forensics soon arrived and cordoned off the factory yard. We three sat in the van wagging our fingers at those crooks saying what a lot of naughty boys you are to do such a thing. Patrick and Dermot would make occasional comments in some strange language that was lost on me. It may have been Gaelic. We were all pissing ourselves as the ring leaders were marched out in handcuffs. It was a time to rejoice from our concealed position.

A few days later I retrieved the blood soaked piece of cloth that I had rescued that day from the gypsum hopper and sent it to the police anonymously. A few weeks passed, Patrick and Dermot were arrested as accomplices to eleven murders.

They were eventually released and no further charges were brought when the police realised that they were just caught up in things by being employed at the cement company. The blood soaked cloth did turn out to be significant and was the lynch pin in sentencing the perpetrators. The main culprits ended up with life sentences of thirty five years each. Patrick and Dermot stayed with me for a few more years in Fiddler Street until the day they decided to move on as was their way. I bade them farewell and told them that I would never forget them.

I did get over the smell and the sheer brutality of this job and ended up working at the Mortuary for the rest of my life. During this time I saw a lot of my old school friends arrive and depart one way or the other. It was a real shit job, but someone had to do it.

www.ingramcontent.com/pod-product-compliance
Ingram Content Group UK Ltd.
Pitfield, Milton Keynes, MK11 3LW, UK
UKHW021050270726
13967UKWH00012B/193